the
ART *of* Fly
· Fishing ·

Mixed rods and reels
on Adirondack map

the ART of Fly Fishing

An Illustrated History of Rods, Reels, and Favorite Flies

by Paul Fersen and Margot Page

COURAGE BOOKS

An Imprint of Running Press
PHILADELPHIA • LONDON

9 8 7 6 5 4 3 2 1
Digit on the right indicates the number of this printing

Library of Congress Cataloging-in-Publication Number 00-131789

ISBN 0-7624-0846-4

Photographs © 2000 by Bruce Curtis

Cover design by Bill Jones
Interior design by Rosemary Tottoroto
Edited by Marc E. Frey
Typography: Adobe Garamond and Gill Sans

This book may be ordered by mail from the publisher.
But try your bookstore first!

Published by Courage Books, an imprint of
Running Press Book Publishers
125 South Twenty-second Street
Philadelphia, Pennsylvania 19103-4399

Visit us on the web!
www.runningpress.com

Thanks to The American Museum of Fly Fishing, Otto Beck Company, Orvis Company, Fuji Films, Mamiya Camera Company, Rita Rosenkranz, Lorraine Gilligan, Gary Tanner, Sara Wilcox, and Sean Sonderman.

Edward R. Hewitt's fly box, photo, bo
and reel he made for Maxine Athert

Introduction

The world of fly fishing is one of water, air, and light. It is brilliant feathers and airy confections that sail weightlessly through the sky. It is graceful arcs spun like a magician's wand above a single angler standing on a mossy rock by a silver river. It is the gusty roar of the ocean or the sweet burbling run of a mountain stream. The world of fly fishing is one of wild fish and the remote places where one can find them. It is about the men and women who have come to the waters of the world for eons, seeking food and sport. The sport satisfies several of our most primal desires: to outwit something wild and by doing so catch dinner. Yet, it has evolved from such primitive origins into the artistic and commercial endeavor it is today.

We hope this book will invite you into the glorious world of fly fishing.

Miscellaneous reels and wallets,
turn-of-the-century.

Mixed flies

chapter one
500 Hundred Years of Tradition: The History of Fly Fishing

*"There don't have to be a thousand fish in a river; let me
locate a good one and I'll get a thousand dreams out of him
before I catch him——and, if I catch him, I'll turn him loose."*

Jim Deren

Daniel Webster rod, photo of Webster,
New York Ball & Handle & Spike reels.

From Survival to Sport

Somewhere, hidden in the mists of time, one of our ancestors witnessed a predator, perhaps a bear, taking a fish. In the dim thought process of instinct and survival, he or she attempted to imitate this food-gathering technique, and "fishing" was born. From that point forward, mankind has developed and nurtured a fascination with our piscatorial brethren and has devised various and intriguing methods to capture them. Yes, the initial fascination toward fishing was based on survival—the need to provide sustenance for oneself and dependents—but somewhere along the way we also learned to enjoy the process, and the art of "sport fishing" began to develop.

"Sport" as we know it has evolved over the centuries from some form of activity necessary to human survival, such as hunting, riding, or warfare. Perhaps the best example of this process is the game of lacrosse. Invented by the Iroquois and called "baggataway," which means "little brother of war," lacrosse was a game created for the sole purpose of practicing warfare. Fishing and hunting are no different; necessary for man's survival, these food-gathering activities have become over time pleasurable pursuits and so, recreation.

"And if the angler catches the fish with difficulty, then there is no man merrier than he is in his spirits."

Dame Juliana Berners, 1450

"Fish in the water are always larger than fish out of the water."

Randy Voorhees, fisherman and writer

" . . . when the lawyer is swallowed up with business and the statesman is preventing or contriving plots, then we sit on cowslip-banks, hear the birds sing, and possess ourselves in as much quietness as these silent silver streams. . ." Izaak Walton, 1653

Each of these evolutions from survival to sport has its own specialized history, and fishing—in particular fly fishing—is certainly no exception. But the art of fishing does have a few specific traits that sets it apart from the other recreations generated from necessity. Of all the sports that have evolved from the need to survive, fishing is probably the gentlest, safest, and most relaxing. Hunting can be arduous in nature and violent; racing or riding horses is far from restful; and war-related sports such as boxing, fencing, and the aforementioned lacrosse are, needless to say, brutal. In contrast, fishing is absolutely pastoral in nature and nearly tranquil. Feudal stress in medieval Europe probably had similar effects on an individual as corporate stress does in twentieth-century America. Fishing was, and is, a compelling antidote for both.

The other compelling reason to fish is the challenge and wonder of reaching into an inaccessible world and connecting with one of its inhabitants. Every creature that walks on or flies above the earth is accessible to us by the nature of our common environment. Fish, in contrast, live in a watery world that limits our access. Accordingly, the evolution of scientific devices and techniques enabling us to reach into the waters and the oceans of the world is part and parcel of the wondrous history of fly fishing.

"To capture the fish is not all of fishing. Yet there are circumstances which make this philosophy hard to accept." Zane Grey, writer

Clinton sidemount reel (top), Meek #44 (foreground),
Hardy (behind).

A Brief History of Fly Fishing

For a number of reasons, the written history of fishing begins fairly late, at least relative to its practice. We know through ancient illustrations depicting fishing and references to it that fishing was practiced as early as the third century A.D. For the most part, however, the evolution of angling was recorded only in the hearts and minds of those who practiced the art.

First, it was a simple matter of illiteracy in Europe. Until the sixteenth century, only those associated with the church were able to read and write. We therefore find many volumes on religion, but few about angling. Ironically, one of the hallowed works of angling literature—and the first to appear in the English language—is widely believed to have been written by a nun, Dame Juliana Berners. Published in 1496, her *The Treatise of Fysshynge Wyth an Angle* remains more than five centuries later a landmark document on the sport of fishing. Perhaps its most remarkable aspect is that, in a sport long regarded as the domain of men, a woman—and a nun no less!—is generally believed to be responsible for one of its most revered pieces of literature.

As literacy increased, so did the number of written materials devoted to fishing. By the middle of the seventeenth century, fly fishing was a popular subject on both the European continent and in the British Isles. Soon the English began to assert their dominance in fishing circles, at least from the literary point of view. *The Compleat Angler* by Izaak Walton is the most famous book on fishing ever written (it was reprinted five times within his lifetime), although his contemporaries and many subsequent scholars might argue about whether it is the finest. Certainly during the seventeenth century, the volume of published books on fishing grew considerably, and the art of fly fishing began to separate itself from fishing in general.

The Eighteenth Century

In the eighteenth century, the sport of fishing took hold and grew exponentially in Britain's North American colonies. A brief look at the northeast quadrant of North America where the initial settlement took place is evidence of the stunningly abundant fishing opportunities available to the colonists. Today's devoted angler can hardly look at the great north woods of Maine and upper New England, the Adirondacks, the Catskills, Pennsylvania's limestone streams, the Alleghenies, and the Blue Ridge Mountains and imagine the

Above: Victorian fly bench full of reels. Opposite page: Victorian fly wallet with Meek #44 reel and Hardy Perfect on canoe paddles.

Preston Jenning's fishing badge, day book, "A Book of Trout Flies," handwritten fly recipe & illustration (original), Billinghurst "Birdcage" reel.

Fly-tying scene with Meisserbach reel c. 1895.

leisurely pursuits. Although the growth of fly fishing cannot be attributed solely to recreational interest, numerous fishing clubs sprang up in colonial cities. For instance, Philadelphia, by the time of the Revolution, had numerous fishing clubs and stores where tackle could be purchased.

The Nineteenth Century

Throughout the early nineteenth century, fly fisherman explored the waters of North America and reported their experiences in numerous journals and sporting magazines. As the sport's popularity increased, so did the demand for better and more refined equipment. The great innovators in fly fishing tackle of this period, such as Orvis, Leonard, and others planted the seeds for what was to become the golden age of fly fishing.

By the end of the nineteenth century, there was very little virgin water left in North America. Westward expansion brought with it anglers who had the unimaginable privilege of discovering the healthy streams and abundant ponds of the American West. Following the Civil War, expeditions to the West for fishing and hunting were commonplace; by late century, fly fishing was firmly ensconced in the hearts and minds of the American sportsman.

The last quarter of the nineteenth century

settlers did anything but fish. The truth is, though, colonists had very little leisure time. What modern anglers must remember is that during the eighteenth century, the very act of subsistence demanded considerable time and effort. Nonetheless, what leisure time the colonists did have was likely spent fishing as it provided relaxation and food at the same time. Furthermore, the gentlemen of the period, unencumbered by the need to grow food and cut wood, had more time for

Above: American reel c. 1900

"Angling has taught me about art, as art has led to interesting theories and experiments in angling. Thinking and fishing go well together somehow."

John Atherton, 1932

Left: English brass and wood reel.
Right: Turn-of-the-century and prior salmon flies.

part of his life fishing the Catskills, recording his observations, and tying flies to make ends meet. In fact, Gordon most likely would have passed into oblivion were it not for John McDonald who, thirty years after Gordon's death, compiled his notes, letters, and articles into a book called *The Complete Fly Fisherman*. This book brought Gordon's legacy to light and, in the eyes of many in the angling community, set him apart as perhaps the greatest innovator and technician ever to step into a stream. Today, he is still quite possibly the most influential and revered individual in the history of the sport.

The Twentieth Century

A graph of the popularity of fly fishing in the twentieth century would show two peaks at either end with a distinctive dip in the middle. When the century opened, the popularity of fly fishing was fast approaching its apex. The great rod makers were thriving; new, innovative reel and tackle manufacturers were producing superior products; Mary Orvis Marbury had compiled *Favorite Flies and Their Histories*; and the likes of Theodore Gordon stalked the streams of America. By the 1930s, the renowned angler Lee Wulff was on the scene; perhaps no one did more than he to define the modern sport of fishing. For instance, one of

also produced one of the most enigmatic and influential figures in the history of fly fishing, Theodore Gordon. In his work *American Fly Fishing, A History*, Paul Schullery writes, "Theodore Gordon has become the central figure in the history of American fly fishing . . . it is from Gordon that the modern tradition is most often said to flow."

Gordon, a tubercular, mystical, and romantic figure, was the first great trout bum. A man who devoted himself—particularly in his later years—to the study and pursuit of trout with a fly, he wrote a significant number of short articles and essays, mostly for British publications. Despite his prolific pen, he was little known, except to his fishing contemporaries. He lived out the last

Above: Orvis CFOs on Trident graphite rods.

Opposite page: Three English rods: Paton, Salter Starbuck, Watson & Sons with Leaonard marbleized

the reasons today's fly rods are generally nine feet long or less is because of Wulff's innovations, and his development of "hairwing" flies had an effect on dry-fly design that still echoes today. Even the ubiquitous fly-fisherman's vest was a Wulff innovation. His wife, Joan, a record long-distance caster and teacher, was one of the first women celebrities in the sport. In fact, one of the most famous pictures of fly fishing in the world is that of the beautiful Joan Wulff casting a fly rod while wearing a ball gown. She still teaches the art of fly fishing in the Catskills.

The advent of spinning tackle in the mid-1930s and the post-World War II boom in the sport of spin fishing took fly fishing into what some call the dark ages. Spinning tackle, which made fishing much easier, led to a general boom in the sport. With the market dominated by spinning tackle, however, the number of fishermen who practiced their art with a fly declined. Nevertheless, the sport's evolution continued unabated. At the beginning of the 1960s, the Orvis Company was a small, out-of-the-way cottage industry owned by Dudley Clarke "Duckie" Corcoran. By mid-decade, although its sales were $500,000 and fly-fishing enthusiasts revered it, Orvis was a company in decline. In 1965, Leigh Perkins purchased the company, revitalized it, and by the mid-1990s sales had grown to more than $200 million.

"Until a man is redeemed, he will always take a fly rod too far back—if it fits."   *Norman Maclean, writer*

Part of the late twentieth-century resurgence in the popularity of fly fishing was the result of "The Movie." Even at the beginning of the 1990s, fly fishermen were only a small segment of the overall angling community. In 1992, Robert Redford took Norman Maclean's wondrous little novel *A River Runs Through It* and created a movie that portrayed fly fishing with such beauty and grace that it touched the soul of the American public. The frantic pace of late twentieth-century American life begged to be slowed. The appeal of standing alone in a great river, surrounded by Mother Nature's wonders, and laying out gentle, graceful casts to rising fish, became every outdoor lover's dream. Inevitably, the glory of the natural world on the Madison River in Montana married the power of the advertising world on Madison Avenue in New York City. The dust soon settled. Many of those who flocked to the rivers and streams after the intense publicity surrounding the film drifted off to other whims and interests. Yet, fly fishing at the beginning of the twenty-first century is once again a solid segment of the sporting life. This heightened level of interest, furthermore, has increased awareness of the fragility of the fly-fishing environment. No one can step from a mountain stream, with its crystal waters tumbling over the rocks, and come away without an appreciation for Mother Nature's gifts. So, although there are more anglers on the streams, lakes, and oceans than ever before, these fishermen have rededicated themselves to the preservation of the canvas upon which their lovely art is practiced.

"Fly fishing takes you to spectacular places and gives you a reason for being there that is far more compelling than just looking at the scenery. You become a participant rather than a spectator, the creatures of the water world become an extension of those things you came about...It is difficult to feel lonely when you are 'out fishin'."

Joan Saluato Walff, outdoorswoman, broadcaster and writer

Fishing in West Arlington with 6'6" Garrison. Reels (right to left): Hardy, E. vom Hofe, Hardy Perfect.

Herbert Hoover's Hardy "Marvel" rod, creel, fly box and leader box.

chapter two
Mechanical Aesthetics: Wood, Steel, and Aluminum Reels

"A line must always be fastened securely to the inside of the spool. If you forget once and a fish strips the reel naked, you deserve several kicks. If you forget a second time, you are not worth kicking."

Eric Tavener and John Moore, 1949

Victorian fly wallet with Meek #44 reel and Hardy Perfect on canoe paddles.

When an angler picks up a quality fly reel, there is a symphony of the senses as the feel of the cool, smooth, machined metal and the sound of exquisitely engineered movement reach harmony. The lack of either sensation immediately relegates the reel to obscurity. An angler will hold a great reel with reverence, turning it over and over in his hand, cranking the handle forward to see how smooth and flawless the retrieve is, and then backward to test the quality of the drag engagement inside. Back and forth, back and forth, changing the drag settings, holding it up to his ear to listen to the click. The sound of the click needs uniform solidity, and a good click to an angler is a comforting note. The slightest hint of "tin" or imperfection in the action, and the angler will set the reel unceremoniously back on the counter without comment.

A reel's beauty can lie in its simplicity just as easily as it can reside in the magnificence of its engineering. Stand a Vom Hofe Peerless next to an Orvis 1874 and the only similarity is the fact they are round and hold fly line. Yet, both are memorable for their contributions to fly reel lineage. In fact, the fly reel offers an aesthetic aspect to the angler's experience that has nothing to do with the actual act of fishing. There will always be a debate as to which piece of equipment is more beautiful, the rod or

Above: Saltwater reel and flies.

Opposite page: 1896 fly-fishing gear—James Livingston's illustrated fly wallet and silk line.

the reel. Unquestionably, the cane rods of the late nineteenth and twentieth centuries are magnificent works of art. But as the reel progressed from early handmade instruments of convenience to the later wonders of design and exquisite machining, they have become as treasured as the rods.

Function versus Form

Perhaps the great paradox of the fly reel is that in fly fishing's purest form, it is a non-essential piece of equipment. Unlike the spinning reel or bait-casting reel, the fly reel plays little or no part in the act of fly fishing until the fish is hooked. With a spinning reel, the angler throws out a weighted bait or lure and draws the line. The reel then imparts action to the lure by retrieving it. In fly fishing, the line is the weight and it is stripped off the reel prior to casting. Only when a fish is hooked does the reel come into play, as the angler reels the fish back toward him. Even then, smaller fish are simply stripped in by hand with the line coiling at the angler's feet. In a New England trout stream, for example, where small native brook trout are the quarry, this method is very feasible.

For fish large enough to make a run longer than the thirty-to-forty feet of line available, the reel suddenly becomes extremely essential. Though no one today would consider fishing without a reel, anglers for centuries did just that. Of the three major categories of core angling equipment for any type of sport fishing—rod,

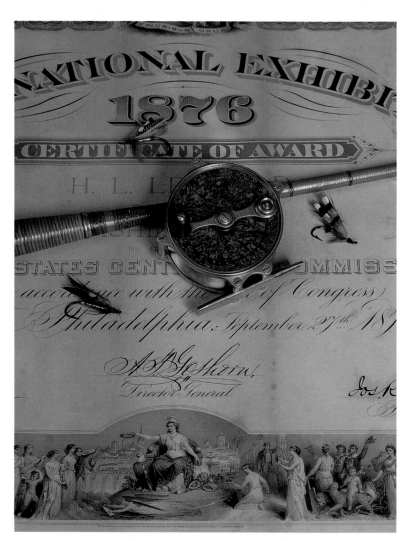

Above: Leonard reel (marbleized) raised pillar (Philbrook patent) on Philadelphia Exposition certificate for rodmaker and 1876 Leonard reel. Opposite page: 1896 reels (clockwise, Herman H. Kiffe Co. nickel silver reel, mahogany brass trolling reel, brass & walnut reel with clamp fitting, Hardy Birmingham reel

Edward Pole, has for sale, at his tackle shop in market-street, near the court-house, Philadelphia, fishing tackle of all sorts, for use of either sea or river, viz. red cedar, hazel, dogwood, &c. Fishing rods, for fly, trolling and bottom fishing. 6.8.10. and 12. Stave pocket reels, furnished with lines &c. Trolling wheels for rock, trout or pearch, with or without multipliers. Bottom layout, and sea lines, cable laid, from large dolphin down to whiting, with hooks suitable from bonettar to the smallest size. Best green or white hair, silk, hardest hempen, flazen and cotton lines, for angling, trolling, deepseas, and other fishing. Trimmers, and man of war trimmers, and snap hooks, with or without springs, for pike fishing. A variety of cork floats in all sizes. Artificial flies, moths, and hackles, with suitable lines of any length. Silk worms gut, in knots and quarter-knots. Best Indian grass.

Salmon, rock, jack, trout and perch, box and plain swivels. Deepseas, with or without swivels for river fishing. Leads made of various patterns, for the use of black point, and other fishing. All sorts and sizes of best kerby and common fish-hooks, ready hung on silk, hair, silk worms gut, grass or Indian weed. All sorts and sizes of hooks, without snooding. Small portable boxes, compleatly furnished, with a variety of fishing tackle. Casting, minnow, landing and scoop nets. Shad, herring and pearch seines. Any person inclining to make their own tackle, may be furnished with any kind of materials

All kinds of tackle mended at a short notice.

Tackle made to any pattern. N.B. As said Pole has now followed the fishing tackle business for several years past, he flatters himself he can furnish the public with better and neater tackle, and on lower terms, than any other in the city.

All orders from town or country will be thankfully received and carefully executed.

A 1777 advertisement for a tackle shop in Philadelphia, owned by Edward Pole.

Creels, English trolling and fly reels

reel, and line—the reel was the last to appear on the scene. The simple hand line was first, followed by the rod—which with line attached offered greater range—and finally the reel.

Before the reel took its place in the angler's arsenal, one of the solutions to the challenge large fish presented was simply to throw the rod into the water when the angler ran out of line. Rod and, one hoped, fish, could be recovered later. Remarkably, Izaac Walton recommended this practice in his seventeenth-century work, *The Compleat Angler.*

The fly reel thankfully offers the angler an alternative to throwing the rod into the water.

Today, fly fishing is practiced in waters of such great size and scope as to change the very

nature of the tackle needed. Once a design of convenience, the availability of the great saltwater fisheries to the fly angler—including the tropical flats, the American east coast estuarial fishery, the Alaskan frontier, and the great blue water fishery for tuna and billfish—has made the fly reel integral to the angler's success. In these fisheries, the power and size of the fish tests not only the rod and the angler's skill, but the ability of the reel. It must hold enough line and backing to allow these great fish to run to exhaustion, and have a drag system smooth enough and powerful enough to slow down the line on its outward journey. At the same time it must protect the line (most importantly the tippet) from

Above, left to right: Wet flies; Orvis reel.
Opposite page: Mixed British wood reels—Nottingham and Birmingham.

All mixed vom Hofe reels on creels.

"Fish! They manage to be so water-colored. Theirs is not the color of the bottom but the color of the light itself, the light dissolved like a powder in the water. They disappear and reappear as if by spontaneous generation: sleight of fish."

Annie Dillard, 1974

any sudden surges that will cause the line to break. Though these jobs are no different from the tasks of any reel in history, the demands on the reel have grown in proportion to the demands of the fisheries.

Early Reels

We begin to see more and more references to the reel—called variously winch, winder, and wheele—beginning in the seventeenth century. The first reels were designed simply to hold line on the rod, manage it, and retrieve it. They were crude as one might expect, and not designed to accommodate a fly line or a bait line *per se*. Through the seventeenth and eighteenth centuries, some wonderful innovations took place, such as the multiplier first introduced by Onesimus Ustonson in the late 1700s. This improvement allowed the reels' spindle to revolve faster than its handle was cranked. Using the multiplier, one turn of the handle equaled any-

Hardy left with Clinton sidemount.

Flies and Meisserbach.

Mixed reels

where from three to nine turns of the spindle. Line pick-up was therefore faster and required less effort. The benefit of this rapid retrieve can be seen today in the fly reel's latest incarnation—the large arbor.

Nineteenth-Century Reels

The fly reel, as we know it today, truly began to take its form in the mid-nineteenth century in Birmingham, England. Known as "Birmingham reels," these reels were very simple devices that were generally narrow-spooled with a curved crank handle and a conventional reel foot. Although not specifically designed for fly fishing, they suited it well. As the Birmingham reels evolved, raised check plates housed the click mechanisms and direct drive handles on the drum replaced the crank handles. This latter development protected the angler from the ever-present problem of the line tangling or catching on the crank handle.

""When you visit strange waters go alone. . . . Play the game out with the stream! Go to it completely handicapped by all your ignorance. Then all you learn will be your very own."

R. Sinclair Carr, 1936

At the same time, another upright, narrow-spooled reel, the Nottingham, was being developed. The wooden Nottinghams evolved over the years into beautiful examples of the reel-makers' art, incorporating dark woods and brass. Though they were not necessarily designed for the fly angler, in their smaller sizes they served that purpose well.

Two American reels also made their mark at this time. William Billinghurst created a rather unique side-mounted reel that offered some innovations that are still sought after today. One important change was retrieve ratio. The Billinghurst reel, patented in 1859, had a very large inner diameter that enabled its inventor to claim a retrieve ratio of "nearly ten times the amount taken up by one turn of the common reel handle." This improvement, along with his ventilation design, made Billinghurst's reel the best contemporary reel for the American fly fisherman.

The second American reel was the Orvis 1874—Patent Reel. Patented by Charles F. Orvis that year and sold until 1915, this reel is the true prototype for the modern fly reel. Orvis 1874's were instantly recognizable, made of nickel silver in their original versions with upright, ventilated spools and built with a crank handle. Interestingly, these reels did well in England where anglers liked the design but found fault with the crank handle.

Orvis saltwater (Lord II) on Orvis saltwater bamboo rod.

Another desideratum in a reel for fly-fishing is that the click should be as light as possible, yet offer sufficient resistance to prevent the reel from overrunning. The friction of the line through the rings and in the water is quite enough, when supplemented by rather a feeble click, to impose sufficient load upon the fish. It is however a matter of the first importance that the line be at all times solidly wound upon the reel, since otherwise snarls will occur and the line refuse to render—always at the most inopportune moment. With too light a click the reel is apt to overrun a little every time the line is drawn out, and this danger cannot be avoided. No music is so sweet to the angler's ear as the whir of the reel, for it announces not only the triumph of his individual skills in tempting the fish to forget their habitual caution, but it promises the pleasure of, and a happy issue to, the coming contest. Though I prefer one which speaks with a crisp, clear voice, though of course this is of no practical value beyond increasing the pleasure of him that uses it; but this it does, at least in my own case, to no small degree.

H.P. WELLS, *FLY RODS AND FLY TACKLE*, 1885

Orvis soon offered a protective rim around the handle to prevent the line from catching.

A third American reel manufacturer of note was Edward Vom Hofe whose family produced reels from the 1880s until just after World War II. The Vom Hofes' contribution to fly-reel design had as much to do with artistry as it did mechanical function. Black rubber sideplates with contrasting nickel silver frames and S-shaped handles set these reels apart as objects of art. Their influence can still be seen today in the work of Stanley Bogdan, Bill Ballan, and other well-known custom reel makers.

In the 1880s, the Hardy Brothers Ltd. in Northumberland, U.K., set foot on the fly reel stage and never left. For more than 100 years they've built a number of great reels, but they are perhaps known best for the Hardy Perfect, a reel that has progressed through a number of changes, but still remains the prototype for classic fly reels.

Modern Reels

The modern fly reel truly is a technical marvel. Many of the best are built with 6000 series aluminum—the same aluminum used by the fighter aircraft industry. The aluminum is finished with a hard anodization process, which

Opposite page, clockwise from top left: Watson and Sons; Hardy Perfect with old English flies; English brass reel c. 1900 with compass; Orvis reel.

makes it both beautiful, and impervious to corrosion. The fittings are made of stainless steel and brass to eliminate corrosion as well. Drag systems incorporate self-lubricating surfaces of Rulon working against cork composite surfaces. There are center-pull drags where the drag system engages directly from the spindle, offset disc drags where the drags connect to the spindle with a gear, and now conical drags where a cone-shaped drag surface around the spindle pushes deeper into a sleeve as more pressure is applied.

Large Arbor Reels

The newest trend in fly reels is the large arbor reel such as the Orvis Vortex, the Loop, and the new Battenkill Large Arbor. These reels enable the angler to retrieve line at a much faster rate than conventional direct dive reels do, and because of their size, they offer significant drag surfaces inside to slow down larger fish. This is a great advantage when fighting a gamefish of great speed who decides to come back to you. When winching a stubborn fish back from 200-

Collection of British trout and salmon brass and wood, late 1800s

plus yards this is even a greater advantage as it reduces the number of times you need to crank the reel. Remarkably this "trend" dates back more than a century to the Nottingham reels and most directly to the reels of Mr. Billinghurst. Why they disappeared in modern, post-war fly reel design is anyone's guess, but they're back and making believers of fly anglers everywhere. Interestingly enough, most modern anglers probably think it's a new concept.

These modern marvels of engineering have enabled fisherman to test themselves with fly tackle against the greatest gamefish in the world. There are gamefish out there that on their initial runs can push a fly reel to RPM levels in the thousands. A shoddily designed reel will simply disintegrate in these conditions, something Mr. Ustonson probably never considered when he built his first winch.

Every angler who has stood on the bow of a flats boat or the bank of a western river and listened to a classic reel sing to him of great fish is forever indebted to a well-designed fly reel.

The great fly reels stay on in use and in collections. The mediocre quickly fade from use and at best end up as oddities in personal collections. One hundred years from now we will look back at the Abel, Orvis, Hardy, Ari Hart, Tibor, Fin-Nor, and Loop reels and marvel at their innovation. Reels that now stand as state-of-the-art in fly shops around the world will eventually stand as museum pieces to be admired for their place in history. What will take their place one can only imagine. It is hard to conceive of anything more advanced than what we use today simply to hold fly line—but undoubtedly improvements will come.

"No pursuit on earth is so burdened by arcane love as fly-fishing, beside which brain surgery and particle physics are simply backyard pastimes."

Charles Karault, broadcaster and writer

Lawrence creel with Garrison 6'6" rod, Hardy reels, and vom Hofe Peerless trout.

chapter three
Willow to Bamboo to Graphite: Arts of the Rod

"Most fishing rods work better if you grasp them at the thick end. If you grasp a fisherman at the thick end, you may get a thumb bit off."

Ed Zern, 1947

Mixed personalities rods: Winslow Homer's Nichols rod and case, Babe Ruth's Hersom rod, Daniel Webster's rod (bottom), Bing Crosby's Orvis rod, Hemingway's Hardy "Fairy" rod.

If you were to put a fly rod into the hands of 100 different anglers, it is very possible you would receive 100 different opinions as to its attributes as a casting tool. Perhaps there is no instrument in all of sports that is as personal as a fly rod. Every sportsman has his or her favorite tool, be it gun, club, or racquet, but the exquisitely crafted fly rod seems to stand above all others with respect to the passions it engenders. There is a very simple reason for this: no other sporting tool is so intimately responsive to its user.

Casting a fly rod is unquestionably one of the most pleasing endeavors a man or woman can undertake. When casting a fly rod, the user is generally in a place of great beauty. Be it western waters of great breadth and scope where thunderstorms dance around jagged peaks, or deep in the great north woods on streams so darkly forested as to seem eternally forsaken by the sun, the pursuit of fish with a fly rod is a remarkably soul-stirring experience.

Function

Rods—simple tools that allows the angler to control the line better than he could using just a hand line—have been used for centuries in the pursuit of fish for survival and pleasure. It enables the fisherman to "reach out" and put the line—and

Above: Combination U.S. rods—1920s, cork and rattan grip.
Opposite page: Daniel Webster rod, marbelized reel, (Leonard) Billinghurst "Birdeagle" reel, Garrison rod.

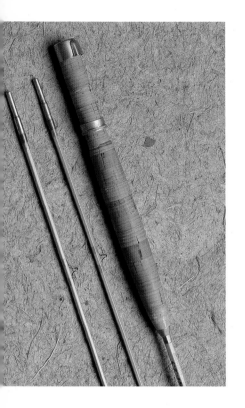

ultimately the bait or fly—in closer proximity to the fish and maneuver it as needed. One only has to go to a pasture pond on a summer day and watch a small boy with a cane pole and a can of worms to know that this fishing method hasn't changed a great deal in hundreds and maybe thousands of years.

The Evolution of the Rod

Just like the small boy who grows and wants to expand his fishing horizons, man's experimentation with the fishing pole and ultimately the fly rod grew as well. In the early days, rods were built of solid wood and often reached lengths of eighteen feet or more. Reels had not yet appeared on the scene and the angler needed the extra length of the rod to help control larger fish. Dame Juliana Berners in her 1496 *Treatise of Fishing with an Angle*, gives explicit instructions on how to build a rod using hazel, willow, and ash. By the seventeenth century, solid Calcutta cane was in use, although not in the split bamboo version we see later.

Through the years, fishing rods were made from a number of other materials. Greenheart, for example, was a solid wood rod that was very popular in its day for its power. Ash and lancewood rods were also very popular solid-wood models, with the ash being used for the butt section and the lancewood used for the tip. Hickory, ironwood, bethabara, Osage, and cedar all had their moments in the sun as rod materials as well, but it was the introduction of Tonkin cane and the six-strip split-bamboo fly rod in the late nineteenth and early twentieth centuries that inaugurated the golden age of fly rod construction. By that time, a number of remarkable craftsmen in the United States were making the great fly rods of the world.

Above: Everett Garrison rod donated to the American Museum of Fly Fishing by Hoagy Carmichael.
Opposite page: Ernest Hemingway's Hardy "Fairy" rod.

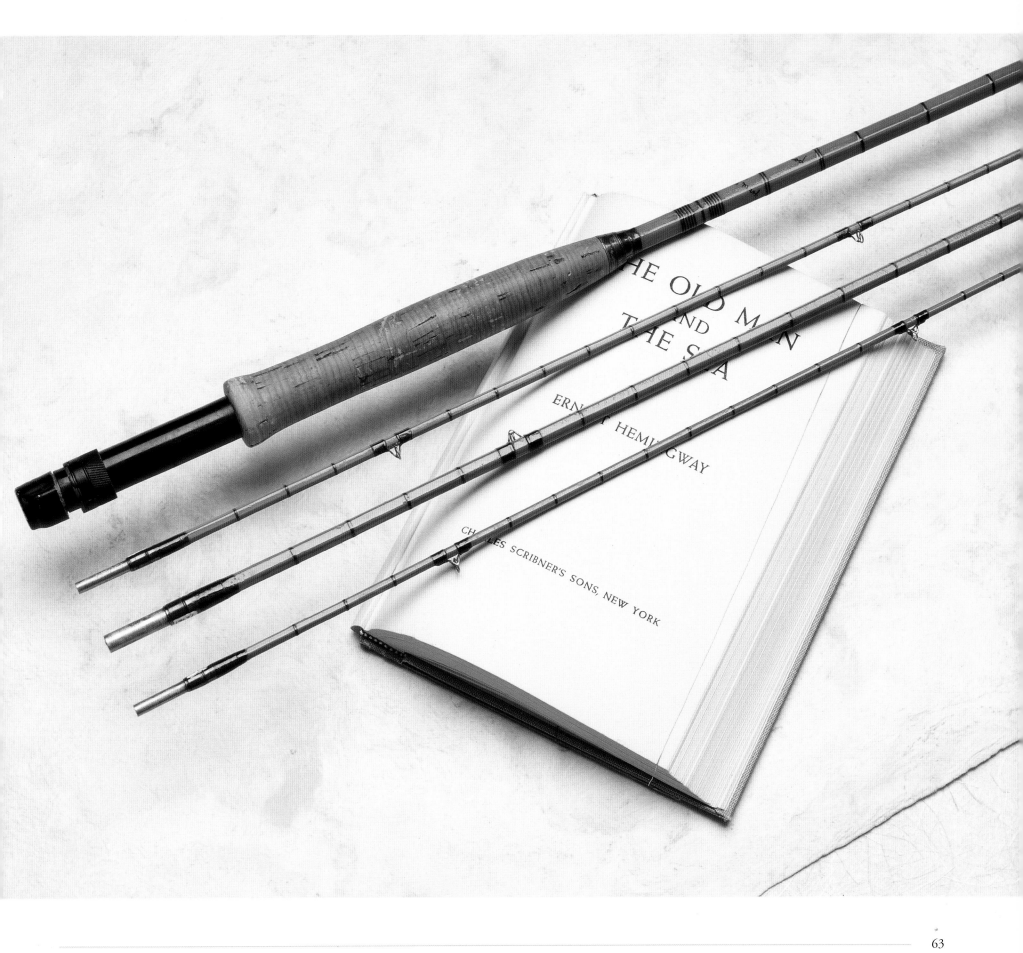

Winslow Homer's B.F. Nichols rod.

"And how you should make your rod skillfully, here I will teach you.

You must cut, between Michaelmas and Candlemas, a fair staff, a fathom and a half long and as thick as your arm of hazel, willow, or aspen; and soak it in a hot oven, and set it straight. Then let it cool and dry for a month. Then take and tie it tight with a cockshoot cord, and bind it to a bench or a perfectly square, large timber. Then take a plumber's wire that is smooth and straight and sharp at one end. And heat the sharp end in a charcoal fire till it is white-hot, and then burn the staff through with it, always straight in the pith at both ends, till the holes meet. And after that, burn it in the lower end with a spit for roasting birds, and with other spits, each larger than the last, and always the largest last; so that you make your hole always taper-wax. Then let it lie still and cool for two days. Untie it then and let it dry in a house-roof in the smoke until it is thoroughly dry. In the same season, take a fair rod of green hazel, and soak it even and straight, and let it dry with the staff. And when they are dry, make the rod fit the hole in the staff, into half the length of the staff. And to make the other half of the upper section, take a fair shoot of blackthorn, crabtree, medlar, or juniper, cut in the same season and well soaked and straightened; and bind them together neatly so that the upper section may go exactly all the way into the above-mentioned hole. Then shave your staff down and make it taper-wax. Then ferrule the staff at both ends with long hoops of iron or latten in the neatest manner, with a spike in the lower end fastened with a running device for pulling your upper section in and out. Then set your upper section a handbreadth inside the upper end of your staff in such a way that it may be as big there as in any other place above. Then, with a cord of six hairs, strengthen your upper section at the upper end as far down as the place where it is tied together; and arrange the cord neatly and tie it firmly to the top, with a loop to fasten your fishing line on. And thus you will make yourself a rod so secret that you can walk with it, and no one will know what you are going to do. It will be light and very nimble to fish with at your pleasure."

Dame Juliana Berners, *The Treatise of Fishing with an Angle,* 1450

Rod-making equipment box—Dicjerson & Garrison rods and Hewitt reel made for Maxine Atherton.

"The indications which tell your dry-fly angler when to strike are clear and unmistakable, but those which bid a wet-fly man raise his rod-point and draw in the steel are frequently so subtle, so evanescent and impalpable to the senses, that, when the bending rod assures him that he has divined aright, he feels an ecstasy as though he had performed a miracle each time."

G. E. M. Skes, 1910

Rod Construction and Design

The list of great rod makers must begin with Hiram Lewis Leonard, a self-made man of many accomplishments. He is credited with perfecting the technique of building the famous six-strip cane fly rod and his constant improvement of ferrule design (the place where the rod is joined), varnishing techniques, and taper design (which defines how the rod is going to cast) are the foundation of modern fly rod design. His company was the cradle of American rod manufacturing and home to some of the greatest rod builders in the world: Hiram Webster Hawes, Eustis William Edwards, George I. Varney, Edward Payne, and George Reynolds at one time worked for H. L. Leonard. Many of these craftsmen went on to form their own companies and create distinguished fly rods in their own right.

No discussion of fly rods is complete without a look at the 140-plus year history of the Orvis Company, founded by Charles F. Orvis in Manchester, Vermont. Beginning in 1856, and for twenty years thereafter, the company primarily built solid wood rods. A number of great rod builders worked for the Orvis Company, the most famous of whom is Wesley Jordan. Jordan invented the process for impregnating split bamboo rods, and making them impervious to the destructive elements of moisture, mildew, cold, and heat that plague fly rods made of natural materials. The Orvis Company also perfected a number of other innovations over the years, including very light rods, and today remains one of the top manufacturers of fly rods and equipment in the world.

Today the era of the split bamboo fly rod is no longer commercially feasible. There are still many craftsmen committed to the preservation of this marvelous art form, but the time and effort it requires is simply too much. Today, graphite is the material of choice and where artisans once created magical wands of cane, engineers now

Opposite page: Leonard marbleized reel c. 1890, raised pillar, Leonard one-of-a-kind rod given by Leonard to Hiram Hawes.

The making of a split-bamboo rod is readily within the accomplishment of anyone who can handle a few of the simpler carpenters' tools, with patience—and your true angler already has this quality well developed. A little time, a little absorbingly interesting work, a small outlay for rod fittings or mountings, and forty-cents' worth of bamboo in the rough is transformed into the most beautiful of all sporting implements, that the owner could not have duplicated by a professional rod-maker for forty dollars. A knife, a small plane, and a file are the principal necessary cutting tools, and with two or three simple contrivances, and one all-important device, these cover the essential instruments.

Almost any manual labor, especially if diverting and concentrating the attention into novel paths, is balm for the jaded or worried mind. This work is light and innately fascinating. How it would have been welcomed by many persons whom the writer has known, while monotonously convalescent from exasperating illness or accident; how it would have sweetened and shortened the days and have proven hypnotic at night for many a weary traveler along the road to restored bodily health and mental serenity. Patients often read and read during a forced period of shutting-in until they can't read any longer, and don't know what in the world next to do to alleviate the tedium of the dragging hours and days. We escaped this experience during an eight-weeks' quarantine for scarlet fever, in beguiling many an hour by winding rod-joints with silk, satisfied that the subsequent coats of varnish preceded by an alcohol bath would prove effectively disinfectant. It was during this incarceration that first we learned of the virtues of pinochle; and the feeling nightly adieu of our teacher Jones, repeated each day with increasing unction, comes back to us as we write these words—the place was the City Hospital: "Thank God! one more day less in the pesthouse."

Not only is the angler's sport, like any other, greatly enhanced by the employment of implements of his own creation, but the very making of a rod is an idyll in craftsmanship, furnishing a recreation salutary and delightful in itself during the wintry days which debar actual but not anticipatory enjoyment of limpid lakes, quiet woodland trails, inspiring mountain heights, merry brooks, and companionable little rivers.

DR. GEORGE PARKER HOLDEN, *THE IDYLL OF THE SPLIT-BAMBOO*, 1920

create powerful rods of high modulus graphite with compound tapers, spending their time experimenting with scrims and resins much the same way their predecessors worked with cane, glues, and varnishes. Rods are tested with electronic load cells to ensure consistency in production and the coatings are cured in ultra-violet light. It's a far cry from the days when shops smelled of wood, varnish, and tobacco.

Today's facility utilizes space-age technology to create its rods, but are far from being mass-produced. Remarkably an element of the craftsmen remains in every rod built. There are still intricate steps in the finishing of a great fly rod that can only be done by hand. It is these steps that maintain the connection between the great graphite fly rods of today and their elegant wood and cane ancestors.

Meer #44 reel (Frankfort, Kent) on bamboo rod, bamboo tip case.

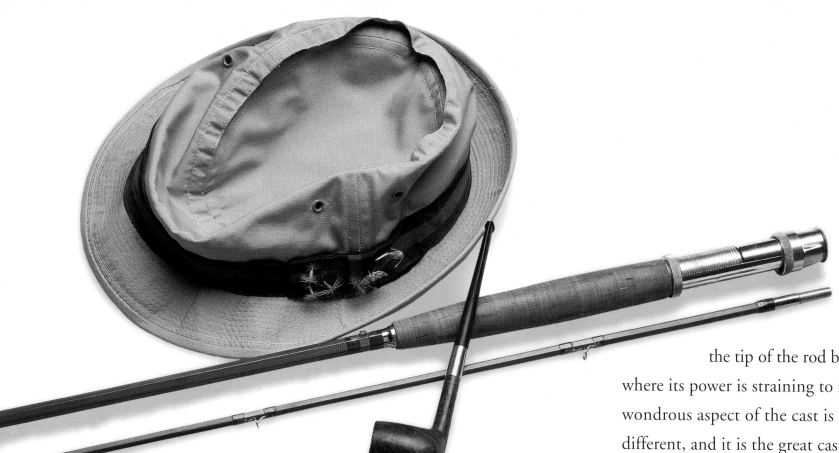

The Relationship between Rod and Angler

Whatever its material, the actual act of casting a rod is rhythmic and wonderfully serene. It is an art practiced in solitude and satisfies that requirement of the soul perhaps better than any other pursuit. Casting a fly rod is a practiced rhythm that comes from an intimate knowledge of the rod. There is no need for force. A great rod needs only to be felt and responded to as it moves through its graceful arc, bringing it forward at the exact moment when the line peels back, pulling the tip of the rod back to that point where its power is straining to find release. The wondrous aspect of the cast is that every rod is different, and it is the great caster who can find that optimal moment in the rod to release its potential. It is this relationship between rod and angler that creates the passions of which we speak. When it's perfect, there's no better moment in sport.

For these reasons, the rod maker's art is revered by all that seek this perfect marriage of man and rod. Once attained, an angler's loyalty to his rod's maker is fierce and he will return time and again to seek other rods from the same source. Over the years the great masters—Leonard, Payne, Orvis, Thomas, and others—created beautifully crafted wands that most certainly caught fish, but even more importantly, stirred their user's soul.

Above: Bing Crosby's Orvis rod, pipe and hat.
Opposite page: E. vom Hofe Peerless trout reel with Krider (Phil.) pack rod.

One only has to peruse the list of luminaries whose hectic and driven lives must have benefited greatly from solitary moments on the stream. We can only imagine the horrors that Winslow Homer witnessed as a wartime artist during the Civil War. Perhaps in later years, his time alone on the stream gave him some solace and inspired his magnificent representations of American country life.

Similarly, Ernest Hemingway's depiction of Nick Adams's time on the stream in *Big Two-Hearted River* is written from personal experience. Hemingway's words could only be written by one who spent time on the water with a great rod:

". . . there is great pleasure in being on the sea, in the unknown wild suddenness of a great fish; in his life and death which he lives for you in an hour while your strength is harnessed to his; and there is satisfaction in conquering this thing which rules the sea it lives in."

Other men of great achievement who chose to spend their leisure time on a stream include Babe Ruth, Bing Crosby, and Presidents Herbert Hoover, Dwight Eisenhower, and Jimmy Carter. These men knew the merits of a beautiful fly rod and used it well.

"At the outset, the fact should be recognized that the community of fishermen constitute a separate class or subrace among the inhabitants of the earth."

Grover Cleveland, U.S. President

Jimmy and Rosalyn Carter's Fenwick rods.

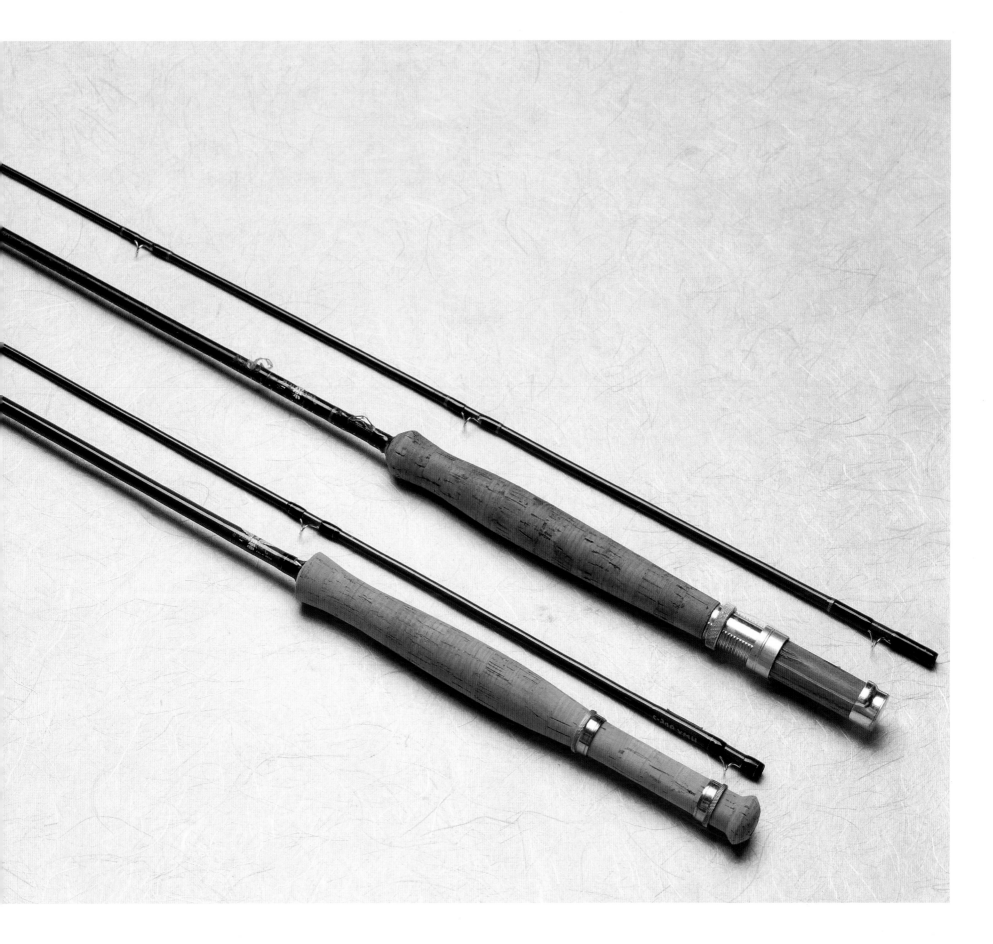

Miscellaneous equipment on Roaring Branch.

chapter four
Natural Artificials: Fly-Tying Magic

"And when you discover that you have tied a killing fly with your own hands, and have made a reluctant trout take it, you will then know the fullness of an intelligent angler's pleasure."

Eugene Connett, 1961

Mix of flies.

Fly tying is an art form

Webster's Collegiate Dictionary defines art as "skill acquired by experience, study, or observation." Instructively, there is no better definition of creating artificial flies for fishing than these seven simple words.

Fly tying is indeed a skill that improves with experience and the study and observation of the creatures and environments we are trying to imitate—insects, streams, and the sea life upon which fish feed. At the same time, fly tying is the one aspect of fly-fishing that can truly be construed as pure art. The proof lies in the number of flies, particularly of the salmon variety, that are tied purely for display and are never intended to drift in a stream and entice a strike from a fish.

Webster's also defines fly as "a fishhook dressed (as with feathers and tinsel) to suggest an insect." The first *Webster's Collegiate Dictionary* was published in 1898; at that time the definition was very appropriate. While it is still appropriate today, a "fly" can now imitate anything an angler wants it to, as long as he thinks it will catch fish. Flies mimic insects, frogs, small fish, bigger fish, crabs, and even mice and small birds, depending on the species of fish sought and its culinary preferences. No matter what the creation copies, it is still considered a "fly."

Mary Orvis Marbury plates.

Charles DeFeo flies.

Fly Patterns

There are references to fly-fishing as far back as the third century A.D. that accurately describe the method by which flies are tied. Aelian in his *De Natura Animalium* writes: "They fasten red wool round a hook and fix on to the wool two feathers which grow under a cock's wattles." From that point forward we can follow the development of the fly-tier's art through the centuries to the myriad patterns that exist today.

Flies or fly patterns are as numerous as the number of people who have ever sat before a fly-tying vise and attached feathers to a hook. There are literally thousands of known patterns that have evolved over the years and probably even more local or personal patterns developed by anglers for a specific region, stream, or particular pool in a stream. Since flies are tied by hand and no one has discovered a satisfactory way to tie them by machine (and, we hope, never will) every fly ever tied is unique. Even the commercial tiers, whose consistency from fly to fly is remarkable, create each fly just a bit differently. For the angler who ties his own patterns for pleasure, this

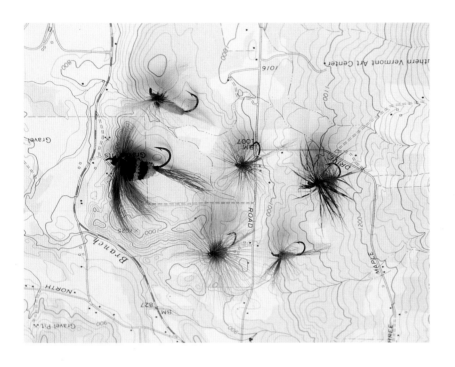

is unquestionably the truth. Perhaps the true beauty of fly tying is that the act of creation is as important and gives as much pleasure as the use of the fly on the stream. Without question, the combination of creating a pattern and then using it to catch a fish is the heart of the fly angler's art and the ultimate joy of the sport.

Trout Flies

For any particular game fish that fly anglers target, there are thousands of flies used to catch them. Certainly the most prodigious type of fly

is the trout fly. To calculate the number of possible trout flies, start with the number of aquatic insects on which trout feed, including mayflies, stoneflies, caddis flies, dragonflies, and terrestrials (grasshoppers, ants, beetles, etc.). Multiply that number by the different stages of their lives (the pupal, nymph, emerging, and various adult stages). Then multiply that figure by the varieties of color and size of the same insect in different

Above, left to right: Saltwater flies from Otto Beck Co.; Streamers; Dry flies on map of Roaring Branch area; Mixed wet flies, English trolling reel with thumb brake c. 1890.

When if an insect fall
(his certain guide)

He gently takes
him from the
whirling tide;

Examines well his form
with curious eyes,

His gaudy vest, his
wings, his horns
and size,

Then round his hook
the chosen fur
he winds,

And on the back
a speckled
feather binds,

So just the colours
shine thro' ev'ry part

That nature seems to
live again in art.

JOHN GAY (1720)

Saltwater flies from Orvis.

geographic regions. Add to this sum the number of tiny bait fish in streams that are represented by flies called streamers. Finally, multiply that total by the number of patterns designed by individuals to imitate all of these possible sources of trout food, and you can see that even Euclid, in all his mathematical splendor, would have trouble figuring out the number possible flies.

There are, however, some standard patterns that have developed over the years that stand as perennial favorites. The Adams (a mayfly imitation), the Coachman (an attractor fly, which is simply the suggestion of an insect), the Irresistible, the Fox Variant, the Hare's Ear Nymph, the Wooly Bugger, the Gray Ghost, Mickey Finn, and the Muddler Minnow are just a few of these. There are a number of anglers who believe that equipped with seven or eight standard fly patterns such as these they can go to any trout stream in the world and catch fish. Whether that is true is not important. The beauty of fly fishing is that you never know what you can do until you step into the water and present your imitation to the fish.

Salmon Flies

Salmon flies represent a whole different approach to fly fishing. Salmon fishing is traditionally practiced when this anadromous fish, in

Top: Salmon flies (bottom is Ballyshannon).
Above: Salmon fly from Bates collection.
Opposite page: DeFeo fly on vise.

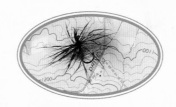

These are the twelve flies with which you must angle for the trout
and grayling; and dub them just as you will now hear me tell.

MARCH

The Dun Fly: The body of dun wool and the wings of the partridge. Another Dun Fly: the body of black
wool; the wings of the blackest drake; and the jay under the wing and under the tail.

APRIL

The Stone Fly: the body of black wool, and yellow under the wing and under the tail; and the wing,
of the drake. In the beginning of May, a good fly: the body of reddened wool and lapped about
with black silk; the wings, of the drake and of the red capon's hackle.

MAY

The Yellow Fly: the body of yellow wool; the wing of the red cock's hackle and of the
drake dyed yellow. The Black Leaper: the body of black wool and lapped about with the herl
of the peacock's tail; and the wings of the red capon with blue head.

JUNE

The Dun Cut: the body of black wool, and a yellow stripe along either side; the wings,
of the buzzard, bound on with hemp that has been treated with tanbark. The Maure Fly: the body
of dusky wool; the wings of the blackest breast feathers of the wild drake. The Tandy Fly
at St. William's Day: the body of tandy wool; and the wings the opposite, either against
the other, of the whitest breast feathers of the wild drake.

JULY

The Wasp Fly: the body of black wool and lapped about with yellow thread; the wings,
of the buzzard. The Shell Fly at St. Thomas' Day: the body of green wool and lapped about
with the herl of the peacock's tail; wings, of the buzzard.

AUGUST

The Drake Fly: the body of black wool and lapped about with black silk; wings of the breast
feathers of the black drake with a black head.

Dame Juliana Berners, *The Treatise of Fishing with an Angle* (1450)

Mix of saltwater flies.

"Fishing always reaches its peak at a time when the bugs are thickest. And bugs are thickest at the places where fishing is best. . .So whenever and wherever you enjoy good fishing you can expect to find mosquitoes, black flies, midges, or deerflies, all lusting for your life's blood."

H. G. Tapply, 1964

land. River names like Cascapedia, Restigouche, Spey, Dee, and Miramichi are siren calls to the salmon angler and represent the high cathedrals for worship of this great game fish.

Since salmon are not particularly interested in eating, it is not necessary that a fly imitate a food source. A salmon fly is designed to draw a strike from instinct or anger. Accordingly, it is the most varied fly in fly fishing. A salmon fly loosely represents a small bait fish in shape, but features brilliant hues and designs that have no relation to what swims in the river. Since no need for specific imitation exists, the liberties taken with and the creativity applied to salmon flies have evolved farther afield from Mother Nature than any other type of fly. Patterns with such wonderfully historic names as Green Highlander, Blue Charm, Rusty Rat, and Undertaker are only a few of the many magnificent flies designed for salmon. There is certainly no food source called a Highlander or a Charm, and Rusty Rat doesn't

order to spawn, returns from the ocean to the exact spot upstream where it was born. When the salmon make this run, they are intent only on procreation. Furthermore, it is believed that when salmon hit fresh water their bodies change and they lose their desire to feed. This is probably why a great mystique surrounds salmon fishing, particularly Atlantic salmon fishing in the great rivers of northeast Canada and Scot-

Edward R. Hewitt's fly box.

Saltwater fly.

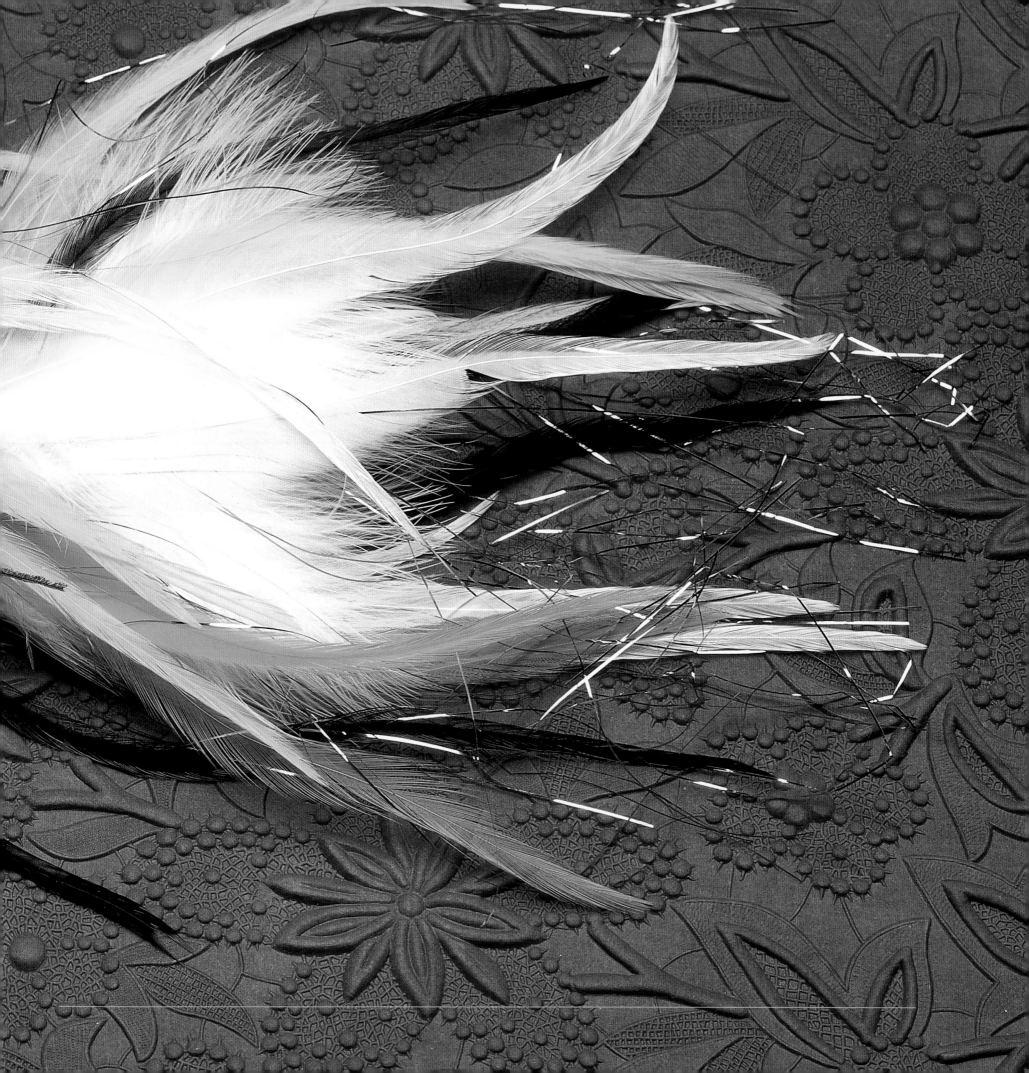

The Bait

Come live with me, and be my love.
And we will some new pleasures prove
Of golden sands, and crystal brooks,

With silken lines and silver hooks.
There will the river whisp'ring run,
Warm'd by thy eyes more than the Sun;
And there th'enamour'd fish will stay
Begging themselves they may betray.

When thou wilt swim in that live bath,
Each fish, which every channel hath,
Most am'rously to thee will swim,
Gladder to catch thee, than thou him.

. . . Let others freeze with angling reeds,
And cut their legs, with shells and weeds,
Or treach'rously poor fish beset,
With strangling snare, or winowy net:

Let coarse bold hands, from slimy nest,
The bedded fish in banks out-wrest;
Let curious traitors, sleeve-silk flies,
Bewitch poor fishes' wand'ring eyes.

For thee, thou need'st no such deceit,
For thou thyself, art thine own bait;
That fish, that is not catch'd thereby,
Alas! is wiser far than I.

JOHN DONNE (C. 1595)

resemble a rat. Remarkably, these flies all have essentially the same profile, but differ in other respects. Classic patterns have very specific recipes and color combinations for dressing, and require certain materials, some of which are incredibly hard to find this day and age. Fully dressed salmon flies tied by the great tiers and mounted for display sell for hundreds and occasionally thousands of dollars.

There is a great difference between salmon flies tied for display (using "dress" patterns) and those tied for actual fishing ("working" patterns). Scotland is responsible for a great many of the traditional salmon fly patterns, and interestingly, the relationship between dress patterns and working patterns seems to parallel that of the traditional Scottish tartans with splendidly colored dress versions and the muted hunting versions in the same pattern. Whether that relationship really exists doesn't matter; it adds more romance to the most romantic game fish in fly angling. There is a time and place for beauty, and a time and place for utility. The salmon fly represents the best of both.

Saltwater Flies

The newest category of flies is the saltwater patterns, mainly because fly anglers have only recently explored the saltwater fisheries. Again, a

Above: Miscellaneous equipment on Roaring Branch.

Charles DeFeo's fly box and sketches.

multitude of patterns exist, but there are a few classics that represent the foundation of saltwater fly fishing; Although classics, these patterns were developed so recently that the innovators that created them are still practicing their art.

The most famous saltwater pattern of all is the Deceiver, created by Lefty Kreh, who still maintains a rigorous angling schedule at age seventy-five. The Deceiver is a large fly that can run from two-to-four inches long and offers a beautiful piscatorial profile of a small bait fish. Normally tied with saddle hackles and bucktail, the variations on this theme are numerous and everyone who ties one adds a little personal touch. Nevertheless, the Deceiver is still and probably always will be the most recognizable saltwater pattern.

Bob Clouser, who is also alive and still fishing, invented the Clouser Minnow. The standard Clouser is very simple in that it offers a bait fish profile, but features weighted eyes that cause the hook to ride upside down and allow the fly to

"Fly making gives us a new sense almost. We are constantly on the lookout, and view everything with an added interest. Possibly we may turn it into a bug of some kind."

Theodore Gordon, 1907

Top: Gar Wood, Jr. Fin-Nor #3 with salmon flies.
Above: Ray Bergman's fly box.
Opposite page: Hardy Brothers flies, belonged to Duckie Corcoran.

sink rapidly to the depth of the feeding fish. Variations on the Clouser are as abundant as the stars in the sky, but if it has weighted eyes and rides inverted—it's a Clouser.

There are hundreds of other patterns, such as the crab and crustacean patterns designed for the tropical shallow water fisheries where these creatures are the food of choice for bonefish and permit. The Crazy Charlie is a perfect example of this type, and represents the foundation pattern of the tropical fishery. The newest members of the tiers' fraternity, saltwater tiers have most opened their minds and hearts to synthetic and high-tech materials to build their creations. Not bound by the relatively tweedy traditions of trout and salmon tying, they use new epoxy patterns to create hard bodies on their flies for shape and durability.

Moreover, materials like Krystal Flash, Flashabou, Ultra Hair, and Prizmatic Eyes are as much a part of their trade as are the natural bucktails, saddle hackles, and the elaborate capes that provide the traditional feathers for trout and salmon flies.

For the innovative fly tier, every fly is a new and exciting opportunity to experiment, refine, adjust, and create. Hours spent at the tier's bench in winter are as pleasing as the hours spent on the stream in summer. The mingling smell of the materials, wood smoke from the fire, and perhaps tobacco smoke from a pipe, conjure memories of pleasant days on the stream, but most importantly, the gentle art of tying offers hope for the future. Every fly tied and placed side by side with its brethren in the fly box is promise of a good fish and a better moment.

"The real lessons of fishing are the ones that come after you've caught the fish. They have to do with solitude, gratitude, patience, perspective, humor, and the sublime coffee break."

John Gierach, fisherman and author

Victorian Fly wallet.

Miscellaneous
equipment with
Adirondack Map

EXCERPT *from*
   TROUT: THE AMERICAN ANGLING CLASSIC

The sun finally passed behind the trees and the pool gradually became in deeper shadow. Then I saw a flash in the water, then another and then came a slight break on the surface. Without getting to my feet I cast my Cahill over the rise but nothing happened. After that I changed flies a dozen times but could not interest the fish although they kept flashing steadily and occasionally broke the surface of the water. Then came a decided smack as one of the trout moved with more speed than usual and I saw the TAIL of a fish appear in the swirl.

"Stupid," I said to myself in disgust. "Those trout are tailing—feeding on the bottom. No wonder the dry fly won't interest them."

I changed the cast to wet flies and tried again. After making some ten variations in the flies of the cast without getting a strike I opened my fly box and spread the collection on a rock.

"Surely," I thought, "there must be something in this assortment which will turn the trick."

I started sorting them over, then picked up one of Walter Grotz's caddis worms and eyed it critically. I knew that this stream was filled with natural caddis and was rather provoked because I had not thought of the lure before.

"You're a bit too white," I said to the tiny artificial, "and a trifle thick. You might work all right in heavy water but in this trickle I ha' me doots."

With the scissors of my fishing knife I clipped the chenille from which the body was made until it was about three-quarters its original size. Then for want of something better I went out to the field near by, picked a dandelion and with the milky juice stained the caddis imitation so that it looked more like the natural.   RAY BERGMAN, 1932

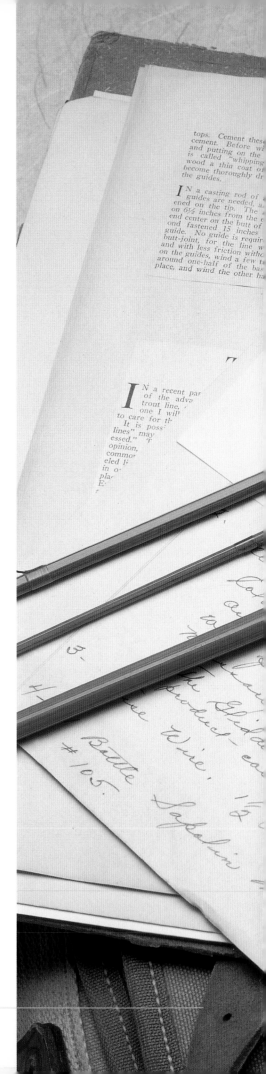

John Atherton's rod, sketches and flies.

Salmon flies with Fin-Nor "Wedding Cake" reel,
E. vom. Hofe #5 Restigouche salmon reel,
Orvis CFO prototype (by Stan Bogdan).

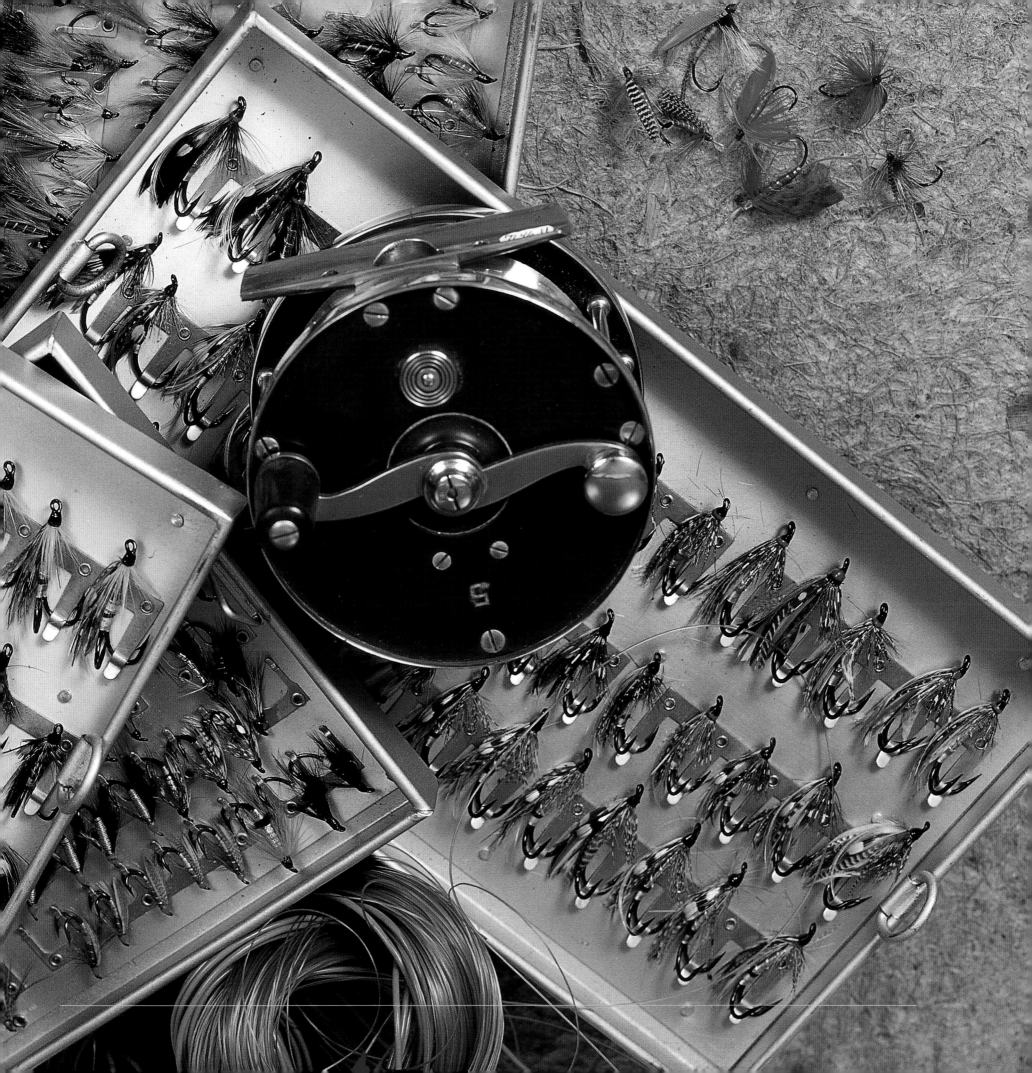

Mixed reels with creel and Orvis impregnated rod.

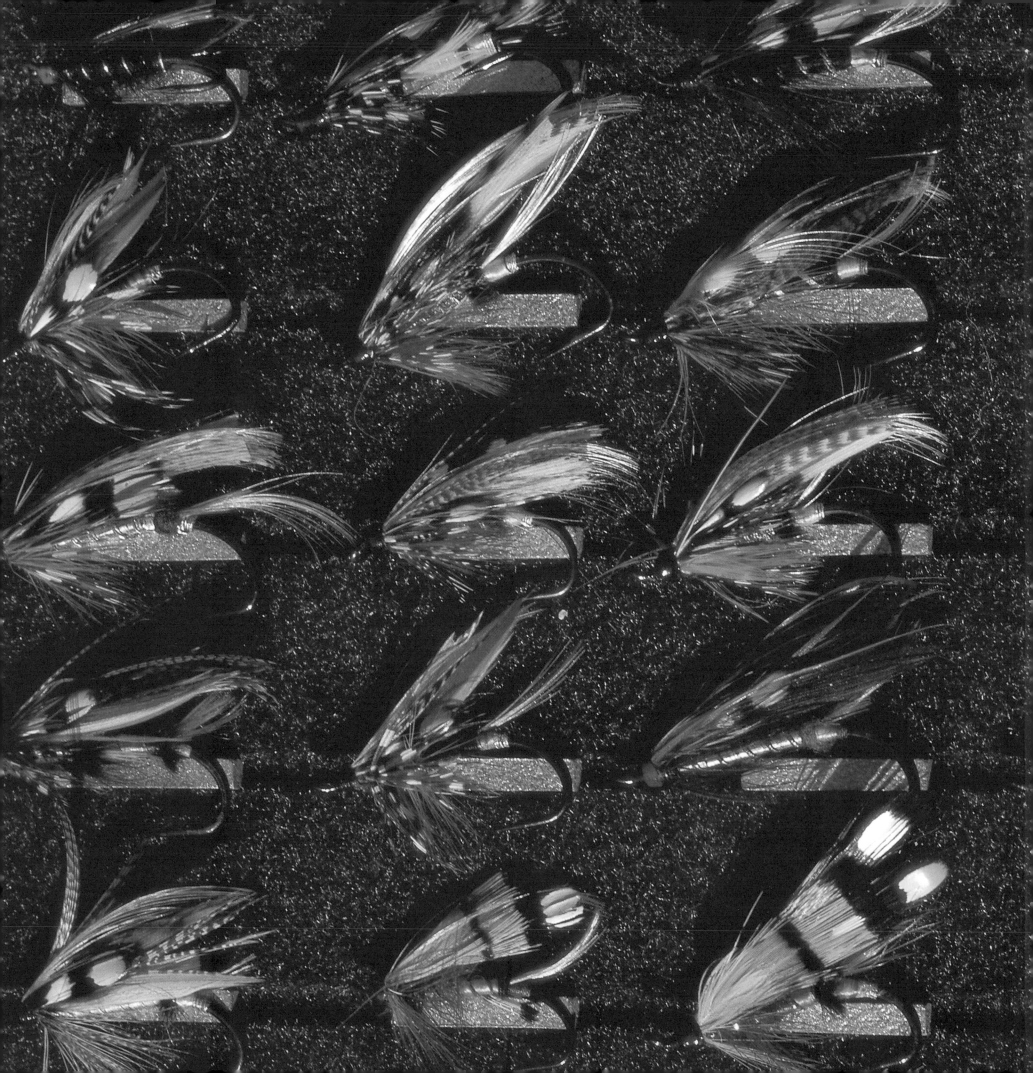